A Thanksgiving Party

by Rosa García

Illustrated by Susan Spellman

PEARSON

Scott
Foresman

Editorial Offices: Glenview, Illinois • Parsippany, New Jersey • New York, New York
Sales Offices: Needham, Massachusetts • Duluth, Georgia • Glenview, Illinois
Coppell, Texas • Sacramento, California • Mesa, Arizona

table

A party will begin soon! The people on the first floor of the Alameda Apartments are having a party. They will celebrate Thanksgiving. Everybody is excited! Every family on the first floor will work together. They all are bringing something to make the party fun and delicious!

tablecloth

chairs

paper cups

paper plates

Sula is from Greece. Sula and her mom are bringing the tablecloths, the paper plates, and paper cups. The tablecloths are decorated with pictures of turkeys, corn, and fruits. They look beautiful!

Kamal is from Lebanon. His family worked with Rebecca and her mom to make the turkey. Rebecca and her mom are from Texas. They are bringing the turkey to the table. It smells delicious!

turkey

Ibrahim is from Nigeria. His parents are bringing apple juice and orange juice and a large salad. The table is almost full! But some people are still missing. More food will come!

salad

juice

Manuel and Martha are from Colombia. They are bringing sweet potatoes and apple pies.

All of the food looks so good!

Everybody is ready to sit down and start the feast.

The lawn beside the Alameda Apartments smells so good with all the food!

After dinner, the lanterns are turned on, and the music starts. The adults dance and sing. The children run around and have a good time. Some of the little kids fall asleep. This is the best Thanksgiving that Alameda Apartments ever had! The people all promise to have a party again next year.

lanterns